I0469812

Basic Mutant Psychosis: Annals of Los Angeles 2014-2016

ISBN-13: 9780692653784

Morgan Drolet

and

Shawn Sullivan

NEON BURRITO PUBLISHING

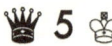 5

Dedicated to Warren Zevon and Jimmy Buffett

Morgan Christopher Drolet

Born in California. Requiescat in pace.

Shawn Michael Sullivan

Irremediable, taking it easy.

Contents

2

0

1

4

I

A mumbling drunk walks by the plaza
Taps the wall twice without stopping
Mumbles on
Standing under Sunset shadow sidewalk sunglasses
She
Drove here from Saskatchewan
Land of living skies
She grew from that place of untamed
A smooth quartz action frame death party with a
wink

II

It's dark early now
Sitting
In the basement of the Hotel Alexandria members of the staff
Because it's Christmas
Are wrapping the leaks on swollen pipes with rags rope and duct tape
Or in the ballroom placing pots and pie tins to catch dripping plaster
Hastily brainstorming treatment for the melting wall paper
Up
Stairs
A young girl allows herself to seep hollow into swimming night
The lobby war games play out to a score by Dylan
An a haggard scrap miner makes a local bet on the horses
From a panhandle phone in roman alcove burning

III

i'm so sorry trumpets are playing
they're noisy
and

i can't ask them to stop
i mean i did ask them to stop
they said i can't ask that from them

IV

his backpack is on his back
his skateboard is on his backpack
his helmet is golden and sparkly
his jacket is royal blue and fits tight
his motorcycle turns left
his street is fairfax to beverly
don't stop that smile

V

Thin faced ol black man on a bike
blue neon wheels flash past
Glitter dripping from Santa hats on mannequin Mel-
rose
Where he slangs the sleigh caps on the go
Burning rubber to a halt he repositions his gear
Almost clobbered by a Chrysler
He shakes his head
watching West Hollywood elementary's student of the
month drive off
An idler in a black mustache pins a pink shadow on a
crippled staircase
With two jackets on
I watch the laughing bare thighs breathing little sex
sighs
Shimmy down the cloistered blvd
As if preening albatross
A steam propelled hangover cloud spurts from wax-
ing philosophical moon
A young drunk upends his guts on the bus
'I guess I drank a little too much'
He spits
All the legs with all their shoes hover
Above the leaking slosh of puke
There's a dog eared ole scamp trying t pawn a hot
pocket watch for a cold drink
And he maneuvers like a grape on a clean white plate

VI

Those days
When we boiled over with careless oblivion
Before the parties had metal utensils and glass cups
When everything was plastic or straight from the bot-
tle
In parks or wooded areas
We'd light things on fire and pluck guitars
We still hated hippies then
In those militant over nothing days
And when you left at night
Us with our dirt still burning
Trophies of empty bottles built in corners
Where did you find us again
Out on the roads
On reds
With cases full of clothes
Where pawned guitars once have idled
Or up about houses
Dry and swaggering on the bluffs
We cast rocks and shadows and demons into the sea
We took jobs as fishermen
Trailing long lines into the heaving green darkness
Sleeping on the sand
With salt spray alarm clocks
Rising with freedom limbs waving
Brushing off centuries old erosion
Or we left you searching
Some under the ground
Others with new masks
Unrecognizable

VII

He always trimmed his nails on the stoop where he
could watch the city breathe
Fritos magazine subscriptions palm fronds
Overflow the trashcan seeping each morning at the
corner
Diamond eyed storefronts wink and shuffle wide
A pregnant riot gurl waddles past in bouncing soles
Her "does your pussy riot?" shirt painted on like eye-
liner
Past Tikum the schizophrenic mute who carries on
his monologues in sign language
He feigns left
BAM!
And he's off like an injured horse

VIII

oops
terrible plan
i'm being honest
everything's pungentish

my soul is the assistant manager
my soul wants to quit
says "enough! beetles
scurry in your heart"

my soul won't stomp my bugs
the bugs won't escape
the bugs will kill my soul
i'm sure my soul will die

no matter what anyone does
there'll be my sadness

IX

"suspicion often creates what it suspects."
c.s. lewis

"oh fuck. is that true? goddamnit. i did it again."
~barry manilow

everyone who will be in this room
is already in this room
the room is paradisiacal,
almost

except
everyone hates me right now

i said the wrong thing
the shift occurred
between me being a guest
and me being an intruder

well there i think i went
so there i go

catastrophes
destroy lives you know
i feel catastrophes because of catastrophes
some which aren't feel like they are
they're different
i can't explain

X

when other-dimensional guests visit
to learn about humans
i won't be a distinguished detail

skip me and fully understand humans anyway
i'm an example of an existence
not the greatest, not the chosen

but, you know
when i go missing, important or not
some of the spectrum goes missing

i'm the kind all twisted and reckless and
wild, whenever possible
that's me and that's the kind i like

you get up to your business
let's chat later
i'm being crazy

XI

one night, a hang thing
zero attendees knew how to start a party
but there was a party

we knew what we were up to
there were stories to drink and listen
madness blossomed
insanity was present
people crumbled
no one minded

like, barry
who treasures sci-fi,
physics, logic, video games,
larping, horror movies,
black metal, net sins,
and terrific breakfast deals
he's with the group
he has his bottle of whiskey
and talks about his vacation to denmark

anthony, gold chained and alive
sits beside emily as long as he can, like two minutes
he drifts away, emily still plays the piano
drew tickles emily's shoulders once, twice
he wonders if emily likes his new jacket
sally stands drinking beer and watching
emily play the piano
emily plays the piano to play the piano
they drink her when they can
they drink when and what they can

none of this is doctor recommended
none of this is good advice
these people are full of malfunctions
they're mapping into destruction
true
but, tell you what
if they have what they create
and what they create is tragic
at least they are having and creating

he snorts coke with thomas in the bedroom
they share things with each other they didn't know
they'd share
the drug does its thing as long as it does
they feel better
they feel worse
they know they feel
they agree they can't count on present moments
moments betray them and they betray moments
they don't know for sure what to feel
they know there is somehow a group thing around
them
wonderful

XII

Two eyes murmur in their wicks
Almost blank with high frequency penetration
The stars seem like loosed olive pits falling
Shouting as they do in voices thick with sweet table
wines and mahogany perfume
Let em fly man
We got our own trip to plan
High stoic shadows of well postured men seemed
stretched
High and thin
from a distance
Planted in spring loaded bucket seats
Bolted above rows of slashing gears in dreaming
They wield the mouths of thrashers trundling over
half golden eaves in hysteria
Keep left at the fork
Keep from under the knife
Keepon ki pinnon
Somewhere traffic keeps time within its I.v. Dripdrip
drip......
And this faucet agrees

XIII

all of us
all 7 billion of us
let's gather together

well, nevermind
that's difficult

hmm, is it possible to
form a global circle
or a kinda humungous box vortex

a crazy shape thing
wow

embarrassing
embarrassing suggestions
ok,

ok, ok. if it's not probable, there's
the party:

walk away at the beginning
for heidegger moments
if those call you

phone people might sit down
and feel comfortable
while eating
with legs curled under their bodies
alone, except not by themselves
persons making make believe
like adolfo bioy casares
a bummer, their fancy dinners
there're such low guest counts
not everyone's invited

persons both imaginative and serious
sad and beautiful
like fernando pessoa
are loved
they can't love back
and they're loved

someone hunts a bear in the front yard
the person doesn't chat much
the pool is full of people
kayaks float down the river

i got a real problem
who's going to eat snacks with me?
nobody!

the snack table doesn't even like me
i'm more like
probably outside smoking a cigarette (of course)
with one person i didn't choose

though you gotta realize
this is also pretend
invite whomever
tiger woods for example
i'm pretending

you can't stop me
you're not invited
you're trying to be invited
you're not invited

(p.s.
crash the party if you want to,
duh)

XIV

Listening to bill collectors ring I
Step out into tolling streets of Spanish Harlem
Just before pavement pops to broiling
With the little white mutt Chanto
Who's loved by the clack nailed PR women with their
breasts like rockets that frighten braziers and the seam
straining thighs
"ay Chanto! Como esta papi?"
The men on stoops gleaming or shaded bronze
Draped in generations down staircases
She told me to have him back quick
To the loft where cigarette fed plants wheeze on the
fire escape
But we're rolling now
Me an this lively mutt
Who stops to sit at a souvenir shop
Pouty lipped pr girl cast of pure sex at 13 feeds Chan-
to a pickle
Slipping her hands across her curves she smiles from
shadow eyes and my heart aches at her artistry
Turning left there's still relics of the old days
The dirty days not sure but true
And the baroque faced mutt leads the way
Back
To the loft with the plants and the girl
Who wants to hang furs in her closet and dance up-
town

XV

people looking at pyramids see
impressive giant tombs

no explanations are necessary

i'm talking about those big big egyptian pyramids
although other pyramids exist
tiny egyptian pyramids
mesoamerican pyramids
the great pyramid of cholula

(
btw,
mayans:
notable artistic success
2012
)

anyway
i don't think one needs to read essays
to like pyramids
you don't need to know quetzalcoatl
or khafra or menkaure or khufu themselves
you can check out their pyramids

cultural foundations
scientific principles
architectural achievements
topics like that
for the essays, the books, for history
i like to see things

that's what i most cherish
i haven't seen the pyramids

this wasn't written while i was in a pyramid
sadly
although
anyone could read this while in a pyramid
recommended

of course what i want is to kiss lee by a pyramid
or just to cuddle with lee while we cruise the gaza
strip in a car

XVI

this isn't a party
oh, this is a party
i'm partly me, you're partly you
we're standing on the balcony
revolving people actions pass by us
i'm pinching my cigarette
you're tapping the banister
you drink your beer you slug your booze
your face turns red you sweat
you tell me everything wrong and meaningless
so i adore you
we know we're meant to be on this balcony
it's the place for us
because we have nowhere else to go
we both know the secret
we visited to talk with others
knowing we had no one to talk with
nothing to say
we know about our blues
we don't really talk about them
we have cigarettes to pinch
booze to sneak inside
we kiss the terrible, as much as we can

terrible things
we adore you
you'll stay terrible for others
we adore you
trying our best here
we're trying our best

XVII

together with you on a random afternoon
we noticed everything terrible about me

when with you the next day
you and i wanted to be free and uncaged and we forgot everything

the day after that we felt uncertain

a week later it was like i never saw you
i felt awful and that was my fault

then i woke up and felt wonderful
because i have to want to

then i woke up and felt terrible
because i'm meant to

later, we ate pizza and mentioned things
i'd been reading gombrowicz's ferdydurke
you'd been reading bolaño's savage detectives
we related to each other's cultural adventures
our minds shared new thoughts

how do these thoughts enter our lives
how does the read become the happening

are we strong enough to do this?
scary question

we wondered and we hoped and what is tomorrow

the world wasn't what we wanted
are we what the world wanted?
we didn't know
the world didn't know
so we agreed
we must keep going anyway
we know we must
we know nothing else except we must keep going
we must keep living
our pizza was tasty

the next day i wrote a poem and said
the world is as bad as it can be or
i'm as scared as i can be
yes, it's the last that's me for sure

i want to funnel myself into culture
find a community
happy to be alive -- alive --- at least

art culture is self-help for the soul
andbut there are so many self-help books
so many with the same theme, of bettering oneselves
everyone can't all be reading the same ones

there are so many different types
the figurative and the literal
the dying on the inside the dying on the outside

i have a real problem
about converting my philosophy into life
converting my thoughts into more than feelings

what i know is
i'm magnetized to those with broken fences
those whose whole front yards have the folk of the
wild
cougars and sloths

wolves and chickens
bears and cats
animals chilling so nice and electric and free
they can be rowdy

i'll know what i can
i'll be rowdy
i'll be so rowdy it'll be like i didn't learn anything
i'll be so free i won't teach anyone anything

since i can't die when i want to
since i can't know when i'll die
i'll live when i want to

you'll always be right
those who are right
you'll never win me
those who want to win me
i got shit to do

XVIII

I skate by on rubber soles
On grey white pools of rippling sidewalk
The red terra cotta tiles seem to slumber bright and
rumbling
The umbrella faces pass at clipped stride on hurried
feet
Girls boots up to the knee
Thud smack! Thud smack!
With scarf colored around their necks dangle swank
and loose or sharp and utilitarian
Me liking it as an insight
Lines of people rake the city blocks for sales
4 dead 75 wounded last count
2 men define mortality in a shoot out at toys r us
The rain swings north
Leaving a trim blanket of chill clear sinking blue

XIX

When the girls dance in the streets
Feet fighting on simmering concrete
Where will you be
When the summoners and thieves are shackled to
their words
(A tin lip squiggled below a nose wriggles)
Will you be in Bradford or New Orleans when the sky
calm and stately blue
Is slowly bundled in canvas flags that mumble causti-
cally jubilant
How resplendent natives weave yesterday masks for
you dreaming
How will you receive them
If in this dream you have no face
But a red russet potato where a face once dwelt
From your window does the moon dawdle
In its half naked glee as it did when
The moors ransacked the country home of dry creak-
ing ancestral dust
Do not tremble in the presents of the hoodoo man
His power
(And he say yours)
Comes from bone
Watch him play the sacred root
Will you wonder at the old way
The whisper days of blood majik
With your eastern eyes set westbound
Can you still bleed a crowd of laughter
In your new chameleon tombs

XX

little bugs scare me
ok, honestly
bugs scare me in general
i know the big ones will wallop me
what will the little ones do

XXI

i thought about the awful
you were there
how do you feel about that?
i think you should feel ok
to be included in my thoughts
just, don't become a nazi
you know
otherwise, it's cool
i'm trying too

XXII

Some stretched out fool on the orange 14 to Alvarado
He's got shoes off
16 crooked toes with three digits each
Throwing Cheetos round like money in a titty bar
And he's falling apart at the seams
Got the dropsies something fierce
This morning some cat on a bike creeps by panning
for change
He's streamlined the operation
The burger stand pinned up
Slowing out with greasy nocturnal nostalgia
The cops across from Linda's Place beer & wine
creep
As the white brick beams green neath or red street-
light
Hanging melodrama 'round the queer Latinos in rec-
onciliation post explosive betrayal
I've got a dull burn for tacos
And the teal eyes staring psychic wafts stale whimsy
from her sheets
Into the boulevard and west

XXIII

I watched a man the shape of a bleeding "s"
Crooked an wobbly from cystic fibrosis
Worn crutches with slippery feet to bolt on his fore-
arms each morning
His complexion a pleading bewilderment
Flashing in stuttering flame headlights
He attempts the long journey from the east bank of
fairfax to the west
drivers lunge at their horns
Their well working feet itching to punch the petals
It's Christmas for Christ sake
No time to waste on this cracked robot hobble
Who sits to rest on cold green bench

XXIV

for a period of time, it's always true --
without your words i am dead
i can't go on without you

at my best i can realize
when i stand crumbled before you
i made the decision
to see myself as crumbled

i treasure when you tell me i'm not crumbled
when you remind me of you as a person
when you remind me of me as a person

but if i'm right about not being crumbled
i shouldn't have to hear it
if i'm right
i'm right in the first place

i'll try to believe that
you can try to push me back to standing when
you want to
because, it's true
i keep going for you
of course
i hope it's obvious

XXV

Chanting ex pats of chemical seduction
Suck at trembling bone china near the limestone
crumble steps of a Chinese haberdashery
Drinking in coffee scented corridors the consistency
of faded sails
Someone's cracking knuckles like a whip
An the boys on the corner dig into deeper pocket
warmth reserves
Beating down the butts and copper and cellophane
crinkle
The grinding whir and smoke electric crowns of
commercial rigs
Jog down endless gasping 3rd st
A hook nosed skirt on the corner drips earrings and
baubles that refract raw molasses like
Wrapt in feathered tinsel
Shoulders oscillate greedily search out a hustle
Eyes painted in mirror match graffiti growth near her
kitchenette garden wall
2nd generation swoll lipped super leeches shedding
lizard breath as he drops into his finances
Grumbling his hand me down problems
Doling out broken promises for broken things to ten-
ants all breaking or broken
A pack of feral patchwork cats whine systematic for
the old wrinkle glazed woman
She feeds them unleavened bread and regales the alley
with her omens of skeletal winged serpents and woe

XXVI

A clean whistle cut and varied through the slices of
city blocks descending
Hey bainey! Gimme a cigarette. But bainey's hand
nods he's busy as he passes
I don't smoke those
That's a woman's brand anyhow
Down the corner stacks
of drums lookin ever like
Like liquor
Stills
Brown rust rings soak down the edge the age
They thud at night like elastic waistbands snapped
against flesh
There's a power line spitting raw electric fuzz
A rubber singe coffee hymn lingers
The kitchen light pops on yellowy at the donut shop
And this puke on the sidewalks gettin me paid to
clean it
Out here the blvd.
on its drop cloth of neon
Pants under the steel eyed stereo night

2015

XXVII

I looked at a picture of you as a child
Blond hair with dark roots
Even as I've seen it
With your smile posed in front of a white
picket fence
I wonder what's in that smile
What happened to you that day
Was your mom
Off to the side of the camera
Watching
The smile looks real enough
You look like a happy kid
But I know times were tough
Back then
Back when your dad left
When that pain was still raw
Each day must have been confusing as hell
Maybe all your actions still owe themselves to
those wounds
I don't like to ask you about it
And I forget sometimes
And I'm a little afraid
And sometimes I feel a quiet sadness
Like today
When I looked at that picture
And wondered about you back then

XXVIII

A middle aged woman in a
Pantsuit
Mary according to the sign
In front of a flower shop
Her arm gingerly outstretched
Trying to stay up wind
Turns spray paints silver the clipped fronds
Off some green tropical behemoth
Lookin like pancaked reptile paws
All dressed up for the holidays

XXVIV

A young homeless Arab in worn socks
lying on the ground
howling clapping
Shaking snakes of oil black hair
Saturated sucking
Sweat
Cheeks exploding imploding
It's an ambitious Louis Armstrong imperson-
ation
Humming acid daydreams
The policeman standing above claps on the
off beats
The muted thwack of his polypropylene
gloves
Saturated
Baby blue
The shutter sing blades of sky above his face

XXX

because of my emotions
being like weather
i find the most comfort on clear and warm
days

los angeles
i'd heard of its 72-and-sunny before i arrived
with the kinda goal in me
a vintage dream that i hope endures

to internalize los angeles
including, neon from nights
since nights i like most, actually

XXXI

this is a secret to my writing that i should
keep to myself:

i pace around like a maniac thinking about
how i want to write
what it feels like to want to write
what it feels like to be feeling

i become lost from the topic of what i was
writing
waste time on myself, wonder about myself
work on myself, work on my adult reputation
when necessary, indeed i also
perform work that improves my adult reputation
then i remember again how i want to write
and i think about what i want to write

then i realize i'm hungry so i go eat a burrito
i drink caffeine i walk to the 3rd street cvs
buy a candy bar, i eat the candy bar
while spinning blocks back to my apartment

XXXII

4pm Christmas Eve
Downtown the streets are warm and blank as
a map
The scene is reminiscent of those early morn-
ings
Wandering through themed Vegas casinos
Their indoor scale buildings and painted sky's
Soundless save the distant whir of a motor
around some corner
I keep putting off the grocery store and its
interminable lines
Where I want to buy a steak for dinner and
leftover breakfast
Beautiful men and women will rain down on
shimmering parties
  tonight
Drinking and laughing on credit
Which will be collected in the morning
Tonight
Transvestites will paint their faces with Holli-
day glow
That may leak off by sunrise
In hollywood the bums in their Santa hats
Red as their faces and just as bruised

Will clang bottles and smoke their Christmas
trees down to yellow fingertips
And I stand
Looking out the turret window of my corner
apartment
Wondering where to go from here

XXXIII

a poem that's a quiet room

with no worries about a clock
and

all those roars outside the room
are imaginary, they don't exist here

to truly be a quiet room
i'll try being quiet to myself because
i scream at myself regularly

so often
later i will again
when i read this. i'll think to myself
"why'd i do this??"
which is the mantra of my life's reflections

[omitted section that said, for example:
this poem is being written past midnight
christmas eve
brett is visiting family in san diego
i'm in a quiet room to write my quiet poem]

XXXIV

His life was like throwing out canvass starting
pleased with the progression so pleased he
found it hard to continue after a point For
fear of ruining what had gone so smoothly
Then pushing forward into a snag Trying
every way to posh through Before discarding
the work and starting anew
She thought about her life as a picture of a
galaxy
Looking thin and splatters
Easily blown awayable
Taken from a million miles away
Through a telescope
Again
Thin and small by scale
But huge when you got right up to it
Unfathomable and unattainable
Full of wandering vessels she couldn't dream
Full and huge
Endless from the inside
Until the knowledge of its edges became reali-
ty

XXXV

this poem happens:

when i'm processing all the things
i've done in a day, and people i've seen

and what i did and who i was
and what that means, and i chew my errors

the thing i try to remember is
i can't regret what hasn't happened
and the worst part would be
not making anything happen at all

XXXVI

She fiddled with her phone
The other hand methodical
Unlacing the rows of tightly packed braids
Massaging the scalp
Beginning on another braid
The massaging must have felt
The way it does
Running a hand through brittle
Matted hair that's been
Crushed motionless by an all day hat
Every so often
At abrupt interval
The woman behind would lapse into a mur-
mur of tears

XXXVII

Old man juggling a bike looking through a wonders
of the world calendar
Getting to the end and starting again
The same 12
Maybe 13 pictures over and over
He's planing his past in expired boxes
Headlined with lush or desolate expanses
Meanwhile just behind him
Young and black but balding
With a picked out fro atop an ever lengthening fore-
head
He's got a red backpack and a box of hazelnut
creamer
Left hand clutching a Spanish onion
The tail of the onion begins to shake
It's a lizard
Opening the box
Reptilian necks begin to crane
Bulging eyes
He shoves the onetime onion ne lizard
No he sets it delicately
In to the dark of the box with its comrades
I notice now
For the first time the one
On his backpack
Nearly glowing green leviathan
Judiciously taking in the calendar thrills
From his perch behind the cyclists shoulder
 And me
 A fly on the wall

XXXVIII

most of my happiness
doesn't come from the world
because the world
doesn't operate on my happiness
a recurring flaw of mine
is acting like an emotional victim

XXXIX

There's the bible then there's me
I'm the fourth God
shut up devil shut up when I'm talking
Tell the truth says the devil
tell me about the number seven
Tell me about the Devils you know
The Devils you've got inside you
Shut up devil shut up when I'm preachin
The bus slowed to a halt
One passenger shouted
Call the police
Then another
Then the same woman again
The driver asked for quiet over the microphone
God and the devil were silent
The bus began to hit its stride once more
Undulating
humming hot with the breath of bodies
God screamed over his radio
Into his radio
Get your butt outta my face
Don't stand so close to me
The devil smiled and bit an apple
Tell me fourth god
He's chewing now
about the number seven
God screamed and rocketed from his seat
His Ox-blood jacket shook with rage
Eyes looked strangled and framed with pain

Cracked black hands
Clench splay clench
The devil stood
Yanking the yellow rope
as the bus came to stop
Merry Christmas he says
no one is dying
 And the devil exits the bus
Merry Christmas said God no. 4
I love you guys
 And God was silent

XL

this is an entire fucking goddamn trilogy about
working at a book store the
day before christmas eve:

a
the woman waiting for someone to finish making her
drink
i see her crying
i have no idea why she's crying
she's just crying
without making a spectacle

i feel like i can relate to her waiting for her drink
with tears
she's a symbol of my feelings about life

b
a red hoodie and black-rimmed glasses and
mascara around her eyes and black hair and
i see a part of myself in
the personality of her eyes
something dark and vicious
brown eyes
anyway

she's come to me and said
she has a list of books she wants me to find
i look at her phone and see dale carnegie's
how to win friends & influence people, which is a
classic

in the self-improvement area, a classic

without even scanning the rest of her list
i'm snotty with her
about looking up her five or so books
i ask her if she needs me to look all of them up

she says yes
she'd like me to look up the entire list

i give her a pen and paper and tell her to write down
the titles
i tell her i'll be back
i head into a section and put some books away
i take a minute

i come back and she's written a couple titles
at the top of the page
in blue ink
she's written
how to win friends & influence people
"ohhhhk" i say, real snotty
and we head out together into the self-improvement
area

how to win friends & influence people isn't there in
paperback
there's a hardcover, i mention there's usually a paperback
i mention paperback is cheaper
i look at her for a moment
she's standing there
we go through the list and a couple books aren't in
stock
one i have to look for it in a different section

i apologize to her for when i was being rude
or annoyed or irritated or, whatever

i say it
i say i appreciate how mellow she is

she stayed mellow
so we both became mellow
she was a bit of hero to me

c
he's a kinda crotchety 25 year-old
tends to complain about things
hates doing things
works a full week of hours
works in all the storer's departments
works a lot and hates it and keeps going

he comes from third floor and gives me a paper
we chat for a second as he descends to first floor
then i look at the paper
with curiosity

on his way through my floor to the third, i ask him
what he gave me the paper for
he says a manager told him to give it to second floor
and i should get the book and call the person

i find the book and wonder about
the procedure for phone payment
i bring the book upstairs
i can't talk to a manager
because there's a manager meeting
i notice the guy from earlier, idly chatting with another coworker

i hold the paper out to him and tell him to take it
he laughs, he looks at our coworker
the coworker makes "a face" and turns away
i remind him he brought me the paper

he shakes his head and laughs
i tell him "i hate how you're laughing at me"
the other co-worker leaves

i say "i'll remember this" while holding out the paper
the paper in his hand, he says "i bet you will"
and i say "oh i will" while walking away

i head to second floor i'm shelving books
from a cart he'd been working on earlier
he comes down and we chat, normal chat
then he heads to first floor

but the big moment comes later
about an hour later, when he's on his way upstairs
and asks me if i'd been upset earlier

i stick my hand out to him
he says something else
i mention my hand
he shakes his head
he shakes my hand

he says something like "because i'm sorry if
earlier…"
i confess to him i also think it's odd i'd gotten upset
i call myself "fragile" today
he makes an "i didn't know if…" comment
i tell him i've already forgiven him

anyway secretly i was glad he'd been stuck with the
paper situation

XLI

thing is, poetry has a bit of a personal problem
a bad reputation
poetry is a total rockabilly nogood greaser

and rockabilly is a keyword for a search engine
in the days of the tech world

the past is a dumpster
i've always found dumpster divers fascinating

XLII

I rode into the city
Arcing up and over the moat surrounding
It seemed to be a gangway
Boarding me onto a great steel vessel
Anchored on the blackening sea
The grey sky brushed breadcrumbs of rain from its
table
The streets raged
With waitresses and stockbrokers and jewelers and
cops and transient acoustic minstrels
In the alleys
And
Down
The steel streets with their masts of glass monolithic
chambers
The dust and smoke blossoms
The city's breath sings past
Like the Mistral through the windows of the chateau
d'If

XLIII

it's easy for me to find another depressive conversa-
tionalist
because many sociopaths
carry a bizarre longing to be listened to
and to debate who currently has the most right to be
upset
or agree on all the reasons to be upset

ready to be
upset any day, any moment
ready to talk about it
ready to overexplain, overstory, overapologize

a non-conversationalist hears
blah-blah-blah
doesn't wanna hear anyone else's story at all
doesn't wanna tell their own

though i think everyone's got a big ol' conversation
going on within themselves

non-conversationalists have the good idea of being
quiet about everything
they put their problems on mute
they don't speak until spoken to
then they say maybe there doesn't need to be so
much speaking

i like quiet times with quiet people
i like loud moments with loud people
and i think that either way
we're all just trying our best

XLIV

down people battling longtime blues
wanna know
who's got the best sass

in an ultimate sense
the best sass is the same as the best of anything
the best last forever

in a daily sense
it's the sound of the sass
hard sass on the right person, in the right moment
when the person was making the wrong thing happen
that's so fucking chill

XLV

you've maybe read another poem of mine
or seen something of mine from cameras
or examined my tinder or instragram
texted me, maybe
listened to my favorite songs
they're your favorite songs too
we share the same favorite food!
you think you got the jist of me

but when you meet me
face to face
on a day not connected with another day
you'll always be one story behind

because the things that make me feel better aren't
always there
+ the things that hurt me come from wherever
whenever they want

i'm a man of emotions and impulses
with mistakes from my emotions and impulses
which later, when i realize the mistakes, if i do, will
make me emotional
and i'll probably do something impulsive
to make up for my previous impulse
i can here and there make a good decision
but, for reasons i can't explain
effects of the good tend to linger for less time than
the bad

so what lifts me up can only lift me for so long

and what crushes me crushes me

knowing the total me, the real me
requires knowing me day by day

might not be worth it, tbh
it's like wandering the beach with a metal detector
a true analogy, for sure, because that's how i feel
about myself
and i'm searching for, like, a long-lost ww2 subma-
rine
even though ww2 didn't happen here
even though the beach is crowded with other people
even though my plan is terrible and unfactual
my buttoned-up shirt has a tacky parrot theme
my shirt doesn't blend with my pastel shorts
it looks like i have a wicker basket on my head

XLVI

I'm slowly stirring Kraft Italian dressing into a bowl
of microwaved frozen corn
There is an empty carton of eggs being
Used as a paper weight
On a stack of ripening bills
We are $783.44 late to Edison
I microwaved the corn too long and the skin has
shriveled like a nut sack
Someone has used the water bill to light a candle
The mismatched lampshades throw bent shadows
mimicking winking eye
Having eaten and smoked a joint
I settle in to
Shit
I forgot my coffee
Here we are
I light a cigarette and settle
Into this sinking couch
With its fabric patterns of bus seat replica design
And crack the spine
Shit
Wheres that fucking ashtray?
Ah
And crack the spine on Anna Seghers
The smoke clinging to the wall sconces
Echoing the mist around the moon

XLVII

anne rice, stephen king
them most of all
because i think h.p. lovecraft and edgar allen poe are
better writers

so i'm talking about the ones who people get nasty
about
those who aren't doing their art right
according to those who wanna be in the know

you don't even realize what you're doing, do you,
critical crowd
you're making them better, truer
by reminding the readers that darkness will always
be around

XLVIII

We watched papillon in the couch and smoked a joint
We fucked in my bed
And after
I lay next to you thinking
"Hey you bastards, I'm still here"
We ate oatmeal cookies my mom had sent for
Christmas
The band bleeding their basement farmhouse fervor
all around us through the stereo
I drank coffee from a red cup
Gilded peacocks and dragons perched on hot clouds
in the enamel
You drank tea
Throat raw from the dry cold of the past couple
weeks
We walked through the rooms
Of my small apartment
Our heavy heels whomping the floorboards
I wrapped your mothers gift with brown paper lunch
bags
The way we did in school
We kissed goodnight
You going back to your mom in the valley
Me going back to a book

2

0

1

6

XLIX

eudaimonia was completed by the first day of
two thousand sixteen
which was, then, the furthest day in the history of human existence so far (fuck yeah)

world population was doubling in half-centu-
ry intervals (holy shit) ! !
at least seven billion people were living ! !
more than ever before (represent)

all numbers were up
including statistics related to
depression, hikikomori, alienation
plus, grave statistics which the news mentioned to keep us informed

point is
people always flip out about their own time

always
and humans are still in their teens
they're not yet both highest volume and furthest accomplished
as they're unable to fully solve an unhappy
problem with having to be human
that's all i'm saying, literally, peace

L

A woman in black uniform
Custodial housekeeping roomservice
Face made golden in the only spray of light
Under the bridge
Up on bunker hill
I watch her
Facing the rising sun
to the east
Her bare arms
    not young
uncovered in warming morning
Los Angeles
I watch her
hold some too small object
Black silhouette lips move
Pray to eastern gods
under the breaking dawn downtown
And she moves the too small object
to her lips
Offers it up and out
Bending at the knees in homage
At the entrance to a parking garage
Under a bridge
Up on bunker hill

LI

A young mother
Daughter's hair of woven pearls
Them running for the bus
Diapers in boxes
       chips dehydrated milk cereal
       non perishables
       files and folders
       plastic dolls
The black wire cart
stacked & secured by expert hands
a full foot higher than the mother's head
Beeping caution of the wheelchair ramp
Lowered
A balancing act up the gangway
Three stops
The scene reverses
A man with hair like Art Garfunkle follows
them with his eyes
Coiffure tingling
in the breeze from an open window

LII

recently i've been desiring to steer my plane
away from an absolute destination

since recently i've been flying my words into
absolute despair

and first of all what kind of destination is despair what the fuck

second of all the flight is the best damn part
jesus christ

so many times i've landed in the wrong
places

it's absurd, in other words i've lived absurdly

which could condition me toward despair

but that's what i'm saying, too, i'm saying
i've still got plenty of gas

and i'm searching for new air traffic con-
trollers in new watch towers

and where i've been and where i thought i'd
go isn't on my mind

two thousand fifteen can rest in piss

LIII

He saw the glint
there
Under the red bench
Below the swift sky clouds
white and billowy morning quick
He stepped off the bus
Holding the turned down brim
the fedora against the wind
Approaching from the rear
Bending
Sliding the quarter across checkerboard square
concrete
Righting himself
Inspecting the printed metal as if
it was the first he'd ever seen
Into a pocket it goes
as the man himself plunges forward
Slowly

LIV

Sitting in my living room (tomb?)
Reading about Piere Renoir on my phone
        https://www.wikipedia.org
Having just read a portrait of him
  painted in the plain poetic words of Carl
Sandburg
So I'm learning about his rheumatism
His death
Always first scanning for the age of the per-
son
at death
Skipping to their final days
Obsessed with endings
I remember my coffee has been cooling
Room temperature being too low
this November
for hot drinks
I read an article
about the people who dismiss
Renoir
and probably others
For a lack of skill or
ability
They're maybe right
I remember a time

Seeming a long time ago
        maybe yesterday tomorrow or later
today
when I thought
        maybe needed to think
that things are better or worse for this/that
Wonder now
Is it just that things are good
for being
this or that
I hear a low incomprehensible voice
Immediately thinking some electronic device
some artificially intelligent operating system is
malfunctioning
Slowly realizing it's only two women passing
the window of my chilly couch
But first I thought it was a robot
The world is a different place now
Different days
than of Sandburg and Renoir
Still
Very much the same

LV

i read about dementia on wikipedia (omg)
i saw myself
FUCK
i became terrified
i considered my psychosis (with delusions of
persecution)
i felt light-headed and intensely worried
i laid on my futon

i remembered how it (wiki) said each symp-
tom of psychosis
and agitation/aggression
must be assessed and treated
independently of the underlying dementia

some long and awful minutes later
i remembered i'm not a doctor and neither is
the internet
and i always overscare myself by reading
medical stuff on the internet
and i thought about a person knowing one
part of himself is altered
a part of him is unknowable to himself

LVI

I am laying in bed now
Woken
Putting on a little Indian music
Barely heard
above the white noise wind
surging funneling whooping
Some bursts punching
Rattling the hunched old structure
around me
The quieting intervals
The gathering of breath
Vishwa Mohan Bhat wafting cresting
stuttering climactic through the room
Reeling in the current
The circuits of air intruding
through the frames of welcome open win-
dows
I am wrapped in bed and blankets
Too lazy warm to venture from this island

LVII

today was mellower because
when i left my apartment i wasn't even
searching for my worries

i ventured into my day without stressing
when people saw me
or pondering if and how other people
thought of me

since anyway that's me thinking of myself
disguised as me thinking of others

and my mission today is to avoid thinking
about myself
since my memories bring my worries

discovering this day as it unfolds
while operating on a neutral, open level

allows the funny to be funny and the sad to
be sad
and all of it, this my life, is nothing to me today but what it is

LVIII

i've decided to think about my life
and this is within my normal routine
of thinking about my problem after it's there
i should have thought about this way sooner

LIX

On a train headed south
through the rail yards
My back painted to the wind
A film crew slips by
Tingle Green paint on an old dodge
skin of an unripe Orange
The camera printed image of tires burning
Black lacerations on the concrete
The bone canal
dry, the LA River
Past a small pond of beached skiffs
Pastel paint chips slowly arching apart
Ditto the chapped leather seats
Cracked rivers and road maps
Creaking June Apollo
Boiling cup of bebop
Pleated ripple of oasis heat rays
mumble on the lipstick rails that
start and end nowhere
The abandoned tracks
like the dead collapsed veins
of the tapioca colored junkie
Who pours himself into a chair
in the shade at their feet
Each time

and at each next station
the train stops
I look down at the tracks
Silent and still
We seem to be slowly sliding backward

LX

i concentrate on the breeze against my body,
which feels as if a mouth blows toward me
a hi top shoe rubs against my right ankle

later i do some reading, but mainly i think
about the writers' lives as filled by their
words
then i wonder if i should stream a movie on
netflix, but i don't

i lie on my futon for no reason but to pass the
time
so a short nap or two sneaks inside my day,
then i eat dinner alone at canter's

then when night comes my worries leave this
world with the sun
and while calmly listening to some of this
year's metal music releases

i read about the united states minor outlying
islands
i google image search the palmyra atoll

at midnight on my day off i feel tired and like
everything's already over

so i go to sleep, planning to wake at eight to
watch wetlands on netflix

except i wake from my sleep once from the
sound of nighttime rain
this confuses my body, which thought maybe
this had been another nap

for some long and lame minutes with closed
eyes i hear sprinkling
until my sleep returns, then early morning
beeps from construction vehicles wake me

so then i have to listen to fucking beeping for
some waking minutes
resulting in me trying to slumber until i rise
to get ready for work again

LXI

This middle aged cat in the fashion district
One leg dangles
       nub 'neath the knee
       like a sausage end
from a wheel chair strapped to a colostomy
bag
Yellow urine hanging in a bent tube
Second leg a scarred prosthesis
He shakes a blue box of baby wipes
rattle crack o' change
Below,
a little dogs head
Panting in the sun
I deposit 50 cents
Happy 4th
Thank you brother
2 doors down from his post
Filling a white styrofoam cup
       black coffee smoke pouring over the
lip
I wonder
Is he a vet
Well, a vet of something at least
Did he lose those legs
in his first foreign land ?

Fighting a war for freedom
he lost ?
When that bomb went off
like a million overzealous fireworks
Took his mobility
Left him to piss in a bag
On a corner
mission in action
prisoner of war for change
I went back
maneuvered another dollar in the kitty
"Good lookin' for ya boy."

LXII

i decided to listen to jay reatard while walking out of my apartment

this decision arrived to me for no particular
reason
just a scroll down musicians in my ipod and
he happened
(a parallel to what will occur within my
thoughts)

in the beginning of blood visions i felt solid
and able to spot qualities that magnetize me
to this musician who died young
he died while he was living

then "nightmares" started playing and my
feelings spun as i heard him sing:
"seems that my dreams only come true
when my dreams aren't about you"

then i thought, he's my dude
we share a fight through this life

so he's dead but alive to me
similar to the relationship he makes me re-
call

LXIII

"Talk to the Virgin Mary man
a One 8 hundred number 1-
800-85555555..."
That smell of distilled alcohol crept
through, around
the December air
I could guess that his black mustache was
soaked
or
maybe a vapor through the pores
Through the clothes wrapped in
layers so thick it was
hard to guess at his actual size
Maybe
he
Never had to trim the 'stache
Just let the high octane spirits nibble
away at its edges
Keeping it neatly clipped above the lip
Who is the talking for when no one's listening?
Is it for the comfort of
knowing he's alive?
If he keeps on strangling the bottle, keeps
on rapping

with only that smooth beautiful glass as audi-
ence
      when no one notices if he's here or
gone
      is frightened by his coming, relieved at
his going
Is this talking as proof, proof enough of
his existence?
Watching him wander off
Slumped
beneath the weight
of backpack bulging zipper seams
maybe we both wonder if he's really there

LXIV

nothing
then everything
then, nothing again
what
ever
that's fucking lame

keep living anyway
got my own reasons for why i'm living
i'd rather be talking about something else
yeah, awkward, my bad

in terms of godzilla
i most cherish the perception of him as a nu-
clear catastrophe
a monster created by humans through the
dangers of science

(this poem is related to me feeling few people
give me reason to keep living these days)
(and i don't give myself a reason either)
(and these problems are related)
(i feel embarrassed, off topic and confused,
sometimes when i talk about this)
(still i keep living, you know, i'm not ridiculous)
(perhaps the only way in which i'm not
ridiculous is i keep living)

LXV

it used to be that i felt life might get hard
then suddenly i'm here in the hardness and i
wonder where life is

my thoughts travel into realms unlike this
world
rather than traveling toward what this world
can be
i travel into the void

wondering when and how i can travel away
from it again
if i have before

LXVI

Sitting on a hard bench
outside of Cabanas Restaurente Salvadoreno
A small grey haired man takes a seat
Juan Ruiz
My hands are cold because it is cold out
Not just for California
but for any hands anywhere
At least sitting ones
I introduce myself at some point later
Juan Ruiz has lost he son
He has gone to see Star Wars
The ticket
For his dead son
was offered by the sons friend
Juan Ruiz took the bus downtown from
Glendale
He missed the 94
Was buying candy as he watched it pass
Through the window of a Walgreens
The bus didn't pass through the window
Juan Ruiz saw it pass on the street
So he took a different bus
Downtown
In an uncrowded "thee-ay-ter"

Watching Star Wars with his dead son's
friends
He has other sons
One in Georgia
Of his four sons
three went to war
The one who didn't is dead now
Another son lives in Las Vegas
Wanting still to "blow shit up"
To quote Juan Ruiz quoting his son
The one in Georgia is a farmer
Chickens, fruits, vegetables
22 acres on which he also raises bees
7 square homes have been built there
In Georgia
For the bees
His dead son was in college
His dead son rode a motorcycle
had a job
was paying for school himself
Juan Ruiz seems sad and proud
Talking about the young man
twenty-4
His love of nature
Climbing and cresting mountains
None of these things killed his dead son
who was riding his motorcycle when
death ripped through him
He doesn't cry
Juan Ruiz
    To strangers at least

Just rings his hands occasionally
They must be cold as well
He buried his son for $15,000
    "It's expensive to die"
in the plot at Forest Lawn Cemetery that was
meant for him
       "You shouldn't have to bury a child"
I cannot argue with that
I cannot imagine that
My mothers greatest fear
for many years
was seeing me put in the ground
We have lost track of time
Him and I
When his bus comes we shake hands
Cold hands a week before Christmas
I watch him
The bright white light of the bus
His patient face
headed back to Glendale
where he will walk 2 blocks home

LVII

then my thoughts shift into another perspective
which rearranges for me the dynamics of my
entire reality

the perspective:
life is not only choosing to be happy
but choosing how to be happy

its deduction:
i often dwell on who i am not
instead of focusing on who i am

i wonder how long this perspective will burn
within me
and if when it goes out i can reignite it

so for a moment considering that i am something
i think, well, that sounds okay
even when i'm not sure i'm considering myself right
but, i mean, i could be thinking about burritos instead
yep, then i think about a burrito because i'm
a little bit hungry

then later i mention this philosophy to other
people
and they stare back at me in silence

so this entire mechanism now worries me

LXVIII

"I used to work for a guy who chiseled wood"
He fumbles with the yellow
   a dirty glowing yellow
mesh backpack on the floor
Nestled between his sneakers

"A wood chiseler"
Trying to hold the large
   3' X 5' wood frame
   missing glass
   backer
and keep his goods
     Also, he chews a long pen shaped
     piece of metal, like a tire pressure
     gauge, missing the gauge parts
Which include a beach towel
A half empty bottle of Thrive cologne
From falling
as the bus comes to a burning halt

"A chiseler of wood"
He is compulsively now
Buffing frame with beach towel
His mouth does not stop
It is moving in union with his hands
Buffing
"Oh shit"

At Alvarado
"Coming through. Driver! Getting off."
Buffing
Maneuvering through sardines of people in
isle of bus
A trout fighting upstream
I watch him
Amongst those other denizens
Entrenched on the corner
Beverly/Alvarado
As he sets the frame atop a sneaker
Lighting a cigarette
Bouncing on ever elocuous lip

LXIX

person: "if you think it's easy being me, you
be me!"
other person: (laughter) "nahh, but for
real..."

a well-known description of me, within the
thirteen people who know me:
my heart is on my sleeve, and fact is i have
low odds for success

so i don't want data sheets but heart sleeves
remedies for my numbers
whatever this means this appears to mean
me
which then also means
many people wouldn't dream of being me either
and i'm like "..."

how many people do i not dream of becom-
ing?

and i'm like, wondering
hmmmm
is it that when one thinks something bad will
happen it does?
can that apply to the good as well?

does one always find the bad in the good and
the good in the bad
and can i focus on the good?

i'll let my yesteryear be a silent film
let it have been made by d w griffith
pretty solid, but we can do better

LXX

Passing a hobo camp
Small
Only 2 tents and a
pile of feeble goods collected
Of one tent I can say
I hardly noticed
Maybe it was green
Maybe that just seems like the
color a tent might be
The other blue
capped with a rain blocker
Violent red
On which read the plea
   "OUR FATHER, WHO ART IN HEAV-
EN…"
Two or several
Maybe more slept
in those tents
this morning 7:53
Or maybe one was a chapel
A place for brothers of the road
Full of sacrament sacrifice songs
from the road
A call for protection
Written on tops of tents
in each camp corner and underpass
Where this city's 26,000 unwilling Franciscans
congregate

LXXI

it's not that i'm obsessed with the concept of
my death
as i'm at least not yet old enough, to be obsessed with thoughts of my own death

what's taking (draining?) my efforts
what's exhausting my emotions (nailed it)
is me trying my damned hardest at being
obsessed with life

so when i talk of life i talk of death
because i try to talk about anything when i
talk of life
which can feel like anything, and sometimes
can feel like death to me
at least i think that, when i glance at skele-
tons or during a bad day or whatever

in the receiving room while working i notice
these books made by other people:
a humorous graphic novel of irrational fears,
titled deep dark fears
vivas to those who have failed, poems by
martin espada
the haunted america faq ("do i believe in
ghosts? no, but i am afraid of them.")
a book on ufos, how to talk like an alien

amid this all sits behold a pale horse

and the cover to the poetry book sentenced
to life by clive james inspires my excitement
makes me realize i'm currently feeling less
alone

these material items with their helpful cov-
ers
imbued with their personal meanings
in them my life feels to me quite realistic
and fantastically electric

here in los angeles i like and miss the mid-
west, with its country emotions
which mean nothing in an ultimate sense
but mean something when you're there and
see them, feel them, live them
(same as most things and places and people)
god i fucking miss feeling like i live around
people
people partially made by trinkets and an-
tiques and country roads
people unafraid of what's outside their
homes they treasure

people with their bucket-hearts overflowing
with endless water (<-- edit?)

[or/and
i miss my youth, as writers tend to]

LXXII

walking to the gas station off Genesee
Smoking
Going to buy more smokes
Which i do
while smoking
It's been like this the last few days
Since the clear beginning of fall
when the weather turned
and it started to feel like drinking
But I'm not drinking anymore
So it feels like fall is now a time for smoking
I smoked weed before leaving the house
I'm tensed up from the cold in two jackets
alarmed by my unconscious tensing
I need to mellow out
This is one of my problems
The weed helps
Sometimes

LXXIII

when you mention the good i might think
you've forgotten to mention the bad
and
when you mention the bad i might think
you've forgotten to mention the good

it's like, what
is nihilism my goal, is that what's happening?
do i hate you, myself, or both of us? what?
both, since we're in the same awful world?
(this part is me being snotty to myself)

sometimes conversations help, sometimes
they hurt
i'm working on not being a hypocrite, by the
way

i keep editing eudaimonia
while monitoring my personal eudaimonic
levels

i discover through writing my similarities to
people experiencing dementia
and learn i'd disqualify as an air traffic con-
troller for numerous reasons

am i as happy as my poems say i am?

well i don't think my poems portray me as
happy
and in this dark moment of admission i'll say
i'm not happy now, not very often
though i feel capable of it, and often find my
reasons for being down ridiculous
and repetitive
and may my moods and thoughts fluctuate
into non-repetitive realms of joy
even during repetitive days

morgan reminded me of our fire within us
when he proposed to me 'eudaimonic' as our
book's title
this word he'd learned as his dictionary
app's word of the day
we chatted about its definition
further inquiry was satisfied through
wikipedia

and, well, i don't know, i don't know
i can say for sure that i don't know
it makes me happy we've completed this
(once read this can only be true)
our third poetry book we wrote together
let this be our year of eudaimonia

still, to be honest, it's still december thirty-
first two thousand fifteen
this poem is set before the first poem, but it's
being written after

here in the final night of this year morgan is
at a show with an old friend
i texted a girl (whom i shouldn't have
texted?) and we chatted fine, and she has a
date
and there's no one one else for me to call
tonight for us to hang
i'll be going into my next year feeling alone
while being alone
what could bring me down is obvious, isn't
it?
i ask the person next to me, as in i'm asking
nobody

because i think i could feel down but want to
feel higher, i get high and look beyond the
obvious

when brett comes home i'm surprised to see
him and
me, myself, i start a conversation with him
about movies
i tell him carol was my favorite movie of the
year
tell him carol is in my heart as mad max is in
the hearts of others
(mad max is in his heart he tells me, yup)

brett tells me the longtime lounge singer of
canter's sings at midnight
she has the last few years he tells me

and i might go, i might not

i don't drink anymore, so bars can bore me,
and i have no real friend tonight
but i might watch a movie, which is where i
store some of my imaginary friends

i'm going to eat dinner at 88 chinese sushi,
it's eight now
i'm listening to black devil disco club's no
regrets, my song of this year
i'm bringing how to get into the twin palms
along with me
i'm thinking about watching juaja later
later i won't finish this poem because the
book is done by midnight
so what i'll do is a mystery to me now

LXXIV

Standing facing the chapel
Corner of Beverly and Liquor
The old man
switching the cane to his left hand as she
reached for his right
          Her blouse succulent red of sin
The other arm pours from his sleeve
caramel and yellow a fist clenched knuckle
white
The bells take up the weight of their silence
Beat it against the belfry walls
Returning it
spent and languid
The way a man finds the first grains of shore-
line and hope
After lost days of shipwreck

More from
Neon Burrito
Publishing, who
deliver the
finest books for
homes and
hearts:

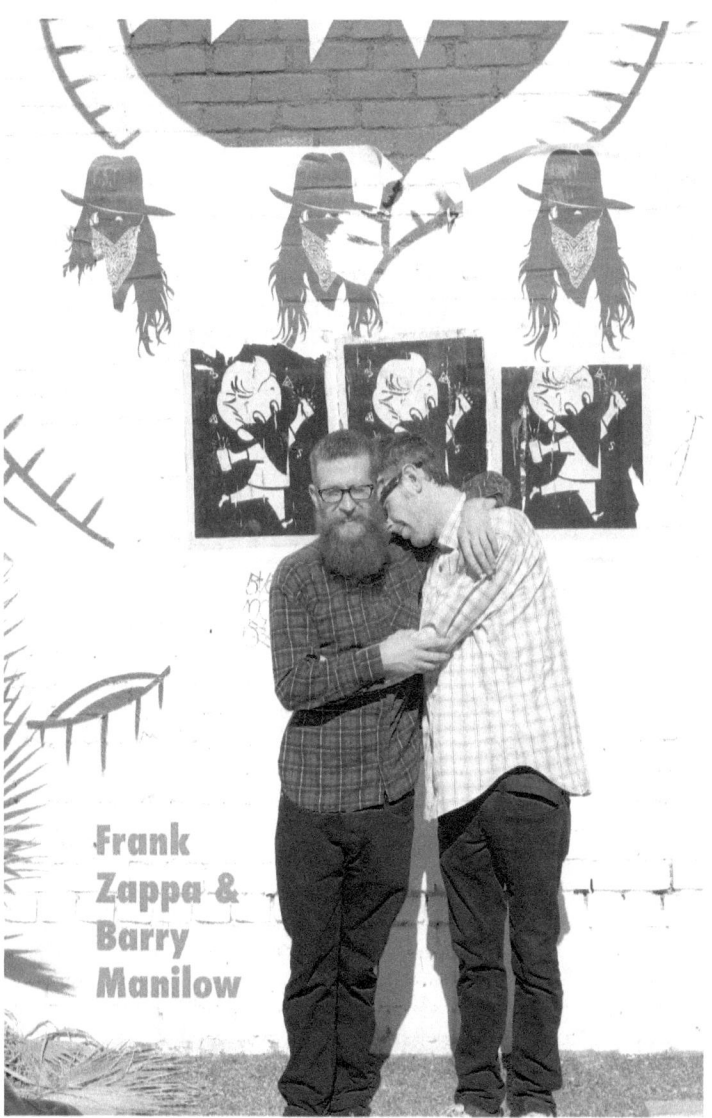

Frank
Zappa &
Barry
Manilow

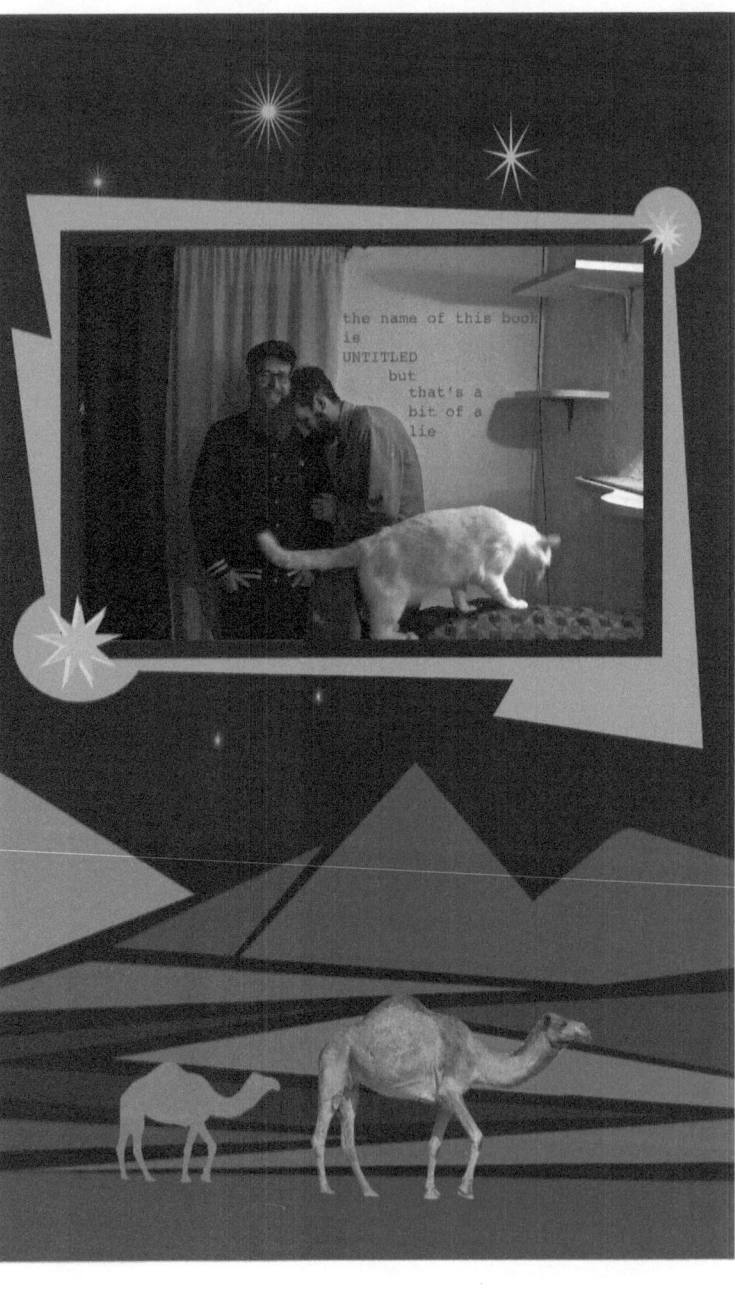

the name of this book
is
UNTITLED
but
that's a
bit of a
lie

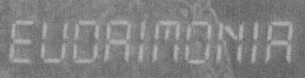

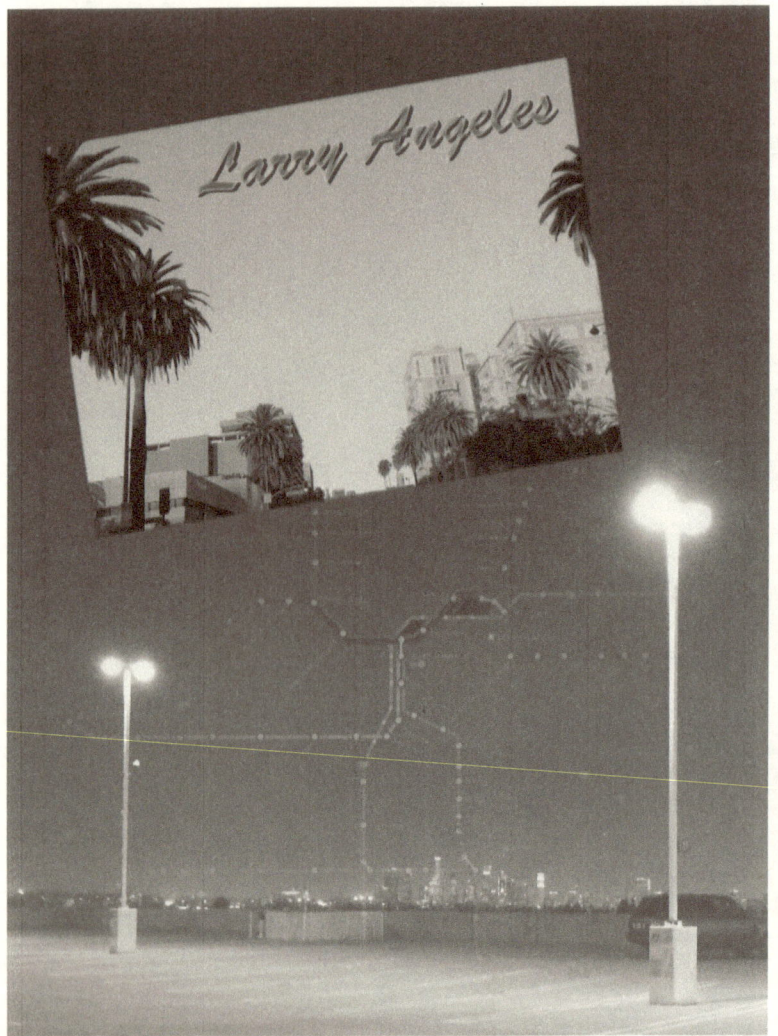

XX